TATTED INNOVATIONS

Helma Siepmann

Translated from German by Etha Schuette

PUBLICATIONS
Berkeley, California USA

This book is a translation of the original German language work titled
KREATIVES OCCHI by Helma Siepmann
first published by Rosenheimer Verlagshaus,
© 1989 Rosenheimer Verlagshaus GmbH & Co, KG, Rosenheim
ISBN 3-475-52624-7

Rights on all samples and tattings by Helma Siepmann
Color photography: Werbe-Design P. Salewski
Black and white photography: B. Lingemann
English translation: Etha Schuette

Publisher's Notes:

Translation from the original German text has been made with the intent of maintaining the integrity of the original work while making modifications as necessary to comply with standard English terms.

Materials have been designated in generic terms reflecting commonly available tools and thread sizes.

The original metric dimensions have been retained. To convert to inches, multiply centimeter dimension by .04 .

© 2002 English text, LACIS Publications
English language edition published by

LACIS
PUBLICATIONS
3163 ADELINE STREET
BERKELEY, CA 94703

ISBN 1-891656-44-9
PRINTED IN CHINA

Forward

Nowadays creativity seems to be of importance for crafters. Be it knitting, pottery, cooking, baking or crafting, everybody likes to be creative. The secret longing to create something special never seemed as intense as today.

I hope that with this book I can offer a new form of creativity that every crafter who enjoys handicrafts can reproduce.

It was important to me to offer a broad view into the manifold possibilities of Tatting Inovations. Because of that, I only briefly touched on the main principles and I suggest that the reader refer back often to the introductory rules.

Once one has understood the main techniques it will become easy to be innovative with your own creations. There are no limits to your own imagination.

The advantage of innovative tatting is that there are unlimited possibilities of combinations of the different elements. They can be freely substituted with each other and you can vary the length of stems just as you wish.

I hope that you will enjoy this new type of handicraft!

Hattingen, July 1989

ABBREVIATIONS

Note: Abbreviations in ( ) are those used in original German language edition.

ds	double stitch (Dk)
ck	change knot (Gk)
Jr	Josephine ring (Jk)
cs	creative stitch (KrK)
p	picot (Ö)
Pr	picot ring (Ör)
sh	shuttle
rs	reverse stitch (Wk)
ct	count (of stitches)
CH	chain
R	ring

Tatting History

Origin, Meaning, and Distribution

Knotting techniques have been known for centuries. As an example think about sailor's knots, weaving and shoemaker's profession. Decorative knotting most probably originated in China and was introduced to Europe (The Netherlands) some 300 years ago.

In Germany this decorative knotting was called "Schiffchenarbeit" (ship/boat work, due to the boat-like shape of the tools). Today it is called "Occhi", referring to the eye shaped rings with picots (following the Latin word oculus = eye). The French call this handicraft "frivolité" due to it being considered needless, a frivolous pastime. In England and America it is called "tatting", in Italy "chiaccherino" and "makuk" in the Middle East.

Shuttles from around 1920

Shuttles from Italy, England, The Netherlands and Yugoslavia

EVOLUTION AND DEVELOPMENT OF TATTING

Initially tatting consisted merely of long strands of knots that were used to form snail – like ornaments for application onto a ground fabric. Later it was discovered that a ring could already be formed on the hand and the first rings were developed.

If one leaves a little space between the (double) knots the tightening of the ring will automatically generate picots.

At first these picots were used just for decorative purposes. Later they were also used to connect rings with each other, thus, their purpose became twofold.

In the mid 19th century tatting experienced a new revival as the possibility of using two shuttles was discovered. The left hand would hold a loop of the first shuttle and thread with the shuttle dangling freely and the second shuttle was used with the right hand to form the knots. Since the loop on the left hand was not led back to the thumb forming an open loop, chains could be worked.

For about a century beautiful new and more intricate patterns were developed. Tatting grew into an elegant craft for the upper society. The graceful movement of the hands while tatting seemed very fitting for aristocratic company. Shuttles became increasingly more valuable. You could find them made of gold, agate, amber, crystal, mother of pearl, porcelains, petrified woods and others, they could be with a gold setting, embellished with jewels or wire decoration.

During both world wars the necessity to knit cuffs and socks for soldiers let the "useless" handicraft of tatting slip into oblivion. In Germany, a renewed interest in tatting occurred only in the mid seventies. Ever since then one can find courses at schools and family education centers that offer tatting.

Tatting could receive a further boost in interest with the technique of innovative tatting shown here. Using a combination of the two known classic stitches, *double stitch* and *reverse double* stitch, I developed a new stitch: the *creative stitch*. It consists of each a half double stitch and a half reverse double stitch and enables the generation of completely new patterns. In addition to that, one does not have to follow given pattern repeats. No more attentive counting and there can be practically no more mistakes. Innovative tatting using the **creative stitch**, offers itself for making flowers, herbaceous plants, trees and much more.

Tools and Supplies

In contrast to the early precious shuttles used, which were a sign for aristocratic wealth, grace and leisure, the shuttles used today are received as more of a practical tool. They are available in plastic, wood and metal.

For innovative tatting one will need 2 to 3 shuttles, small scissors and a crochet hook that is compatible with the thickness of the thread.

The tips of the shuttles need to be tight so that the thread does not constantly unwind when they dangle down. If they are too close together one can correct that by means of a nail file.

Any of the available threads can be used for innovative tatting. The patterns shown in this book were worked exclusively with perle cotton size 8 (except for the two center pieces on pages 64 and 65). This is the preferred quality and size thread to work table decorations. Also, there are many colors available in this thread. Recommended are the variegated/overdyed threads as these enable a color play of natural appearance.

Fabric blends that are easy care for hand or machine-wash and of medium weave should be the choice for ground fabrics.

Ironing: iron first from the top, then again (if possible with steam) from the back side.

Commercially available tatting shuttles

The Technique

Using the Shuttle

Push the thread through the hole in the post of the shuttle and tie it into a knot. Now wind your shuttle full with thread.

The shuttle has to be moved in a flat position, not upright. The thread between left and right hand should not be longer than ca 15 cm.

Formation of the Knots and Elements

ds The photographs 1 – 6 show how to hold the hands during formation of the first, the left half of the double knot, photographs 7 – 10 show the second half, the right half of the double knot.

Here the positioning of the left middle finger is of utmost importance, because this will regulate the tension on the thread. (see photograph 5 and 6).

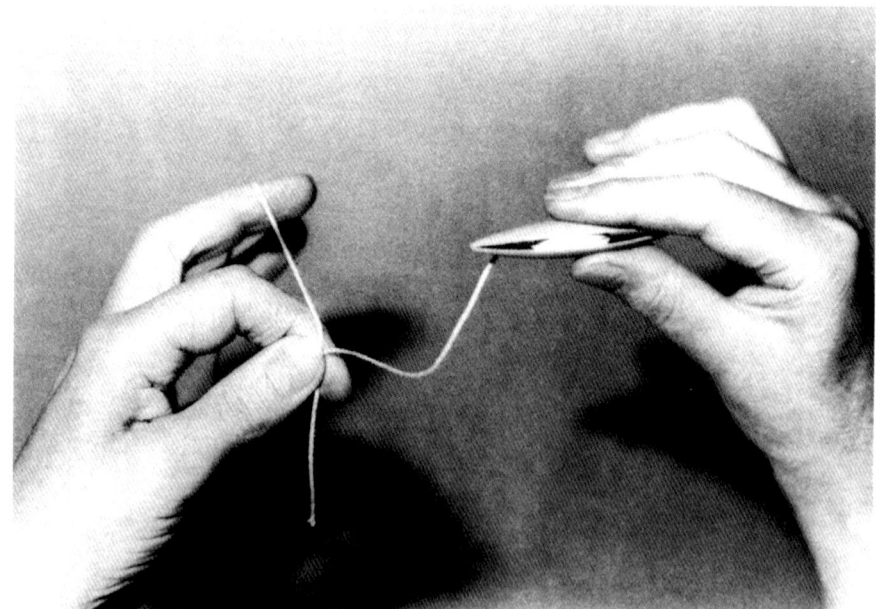

1 Grab the thread between thumb and forefinger of the left hand and lead it back to the thumb over the tip of your finger. Hold the shuttle in your right hand in a way so that the thread comes out from the front of the shuttle and away from your body.

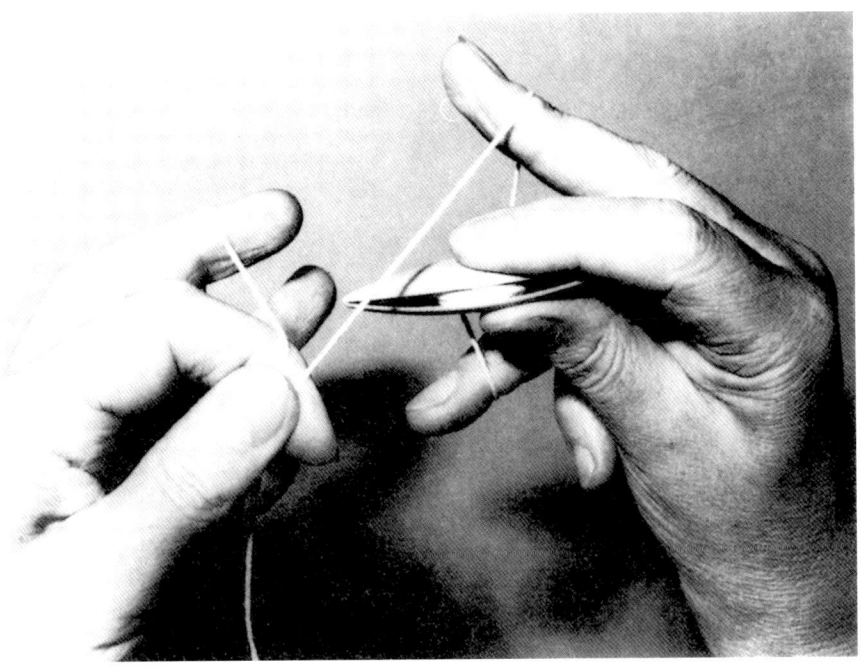

2 Now hold the thread back with your right ring finger and up with the middle finger.

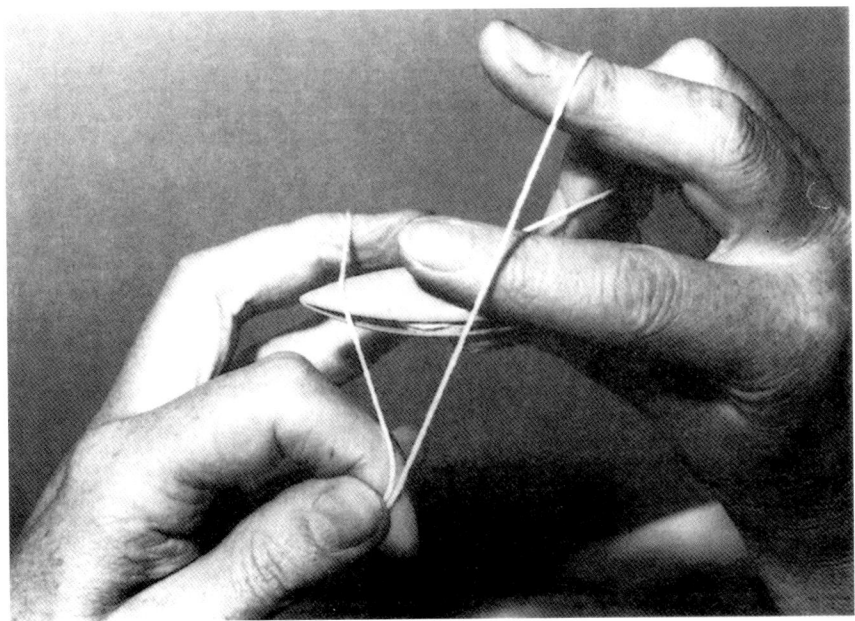

3 Lead the shuttle going under the tensioned thread bridge of the left hand to the left and…

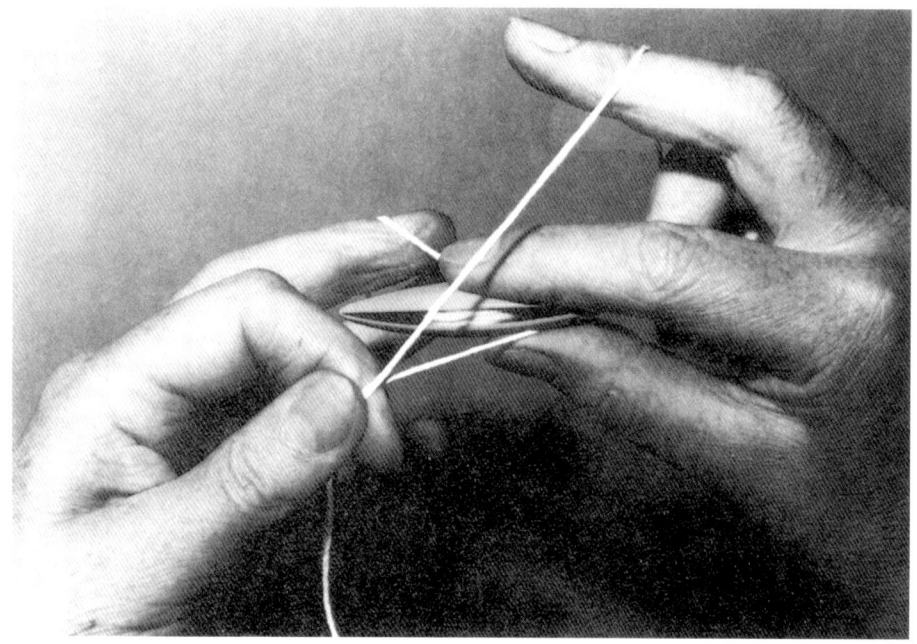

4 ... back over the thread without letting go of the shuttle. The thread will glide through between thumb and shuttle.

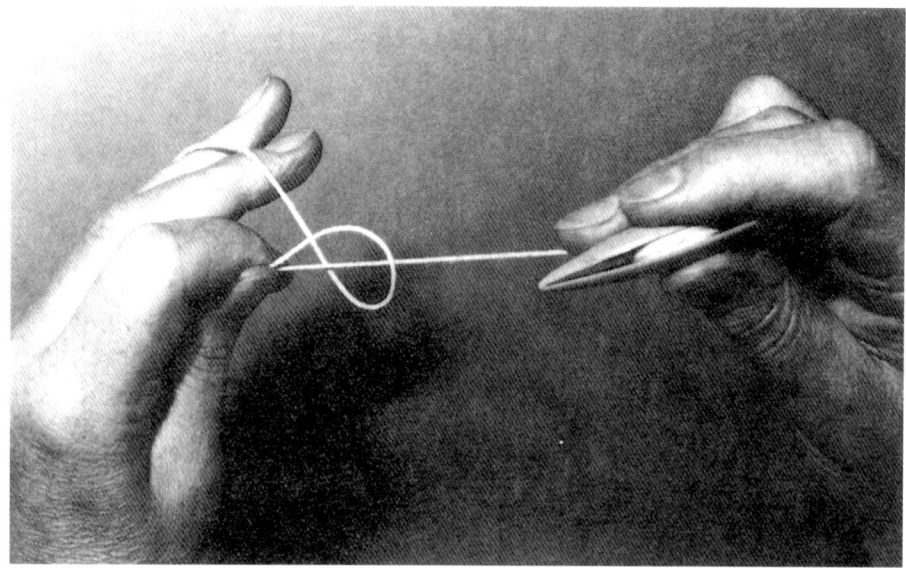

5 Release the tension of the ring of thread that is on your left hand. Only now move the shuttle back towards the right. When the shuttle thread is pulled taught now, the knot on the ring will flip over and transfer to the ring.

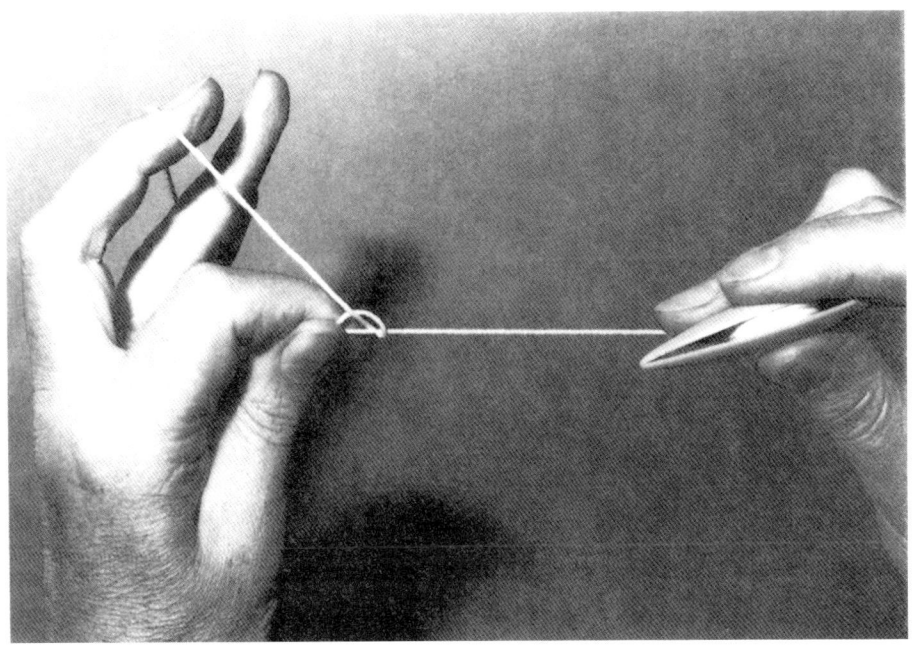

6 Now lift the middle finger of your left hand and herewith move the loop under your thumb. – Very important: keep the tension on your shuttle thread until you have slid the knot under your thumb. Hold on to the knot!

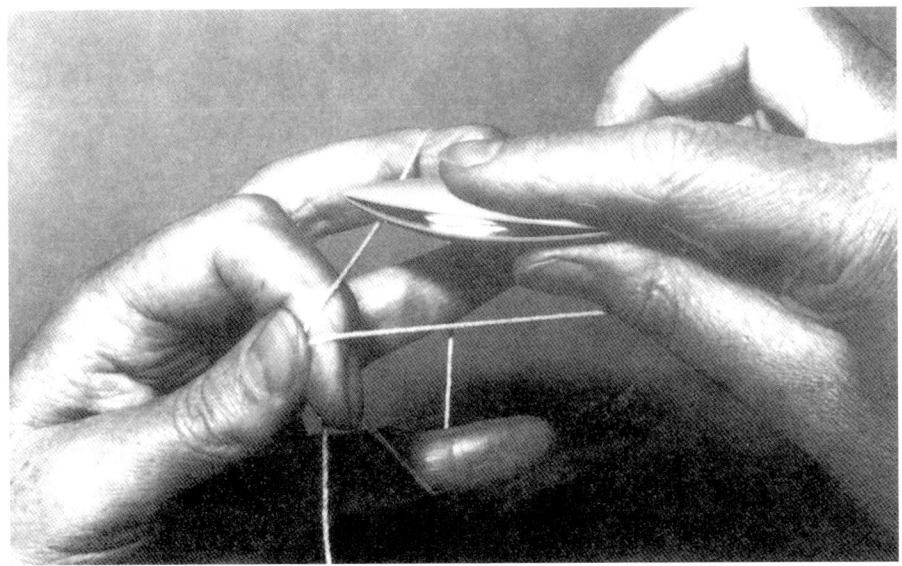

7 For the second half of the double knot lead the shuttle in the opposite way around the thread bridge of the left hand, that is, from the top to the bottom. Take the shuttle thread back with the ring finger of your right hand and put

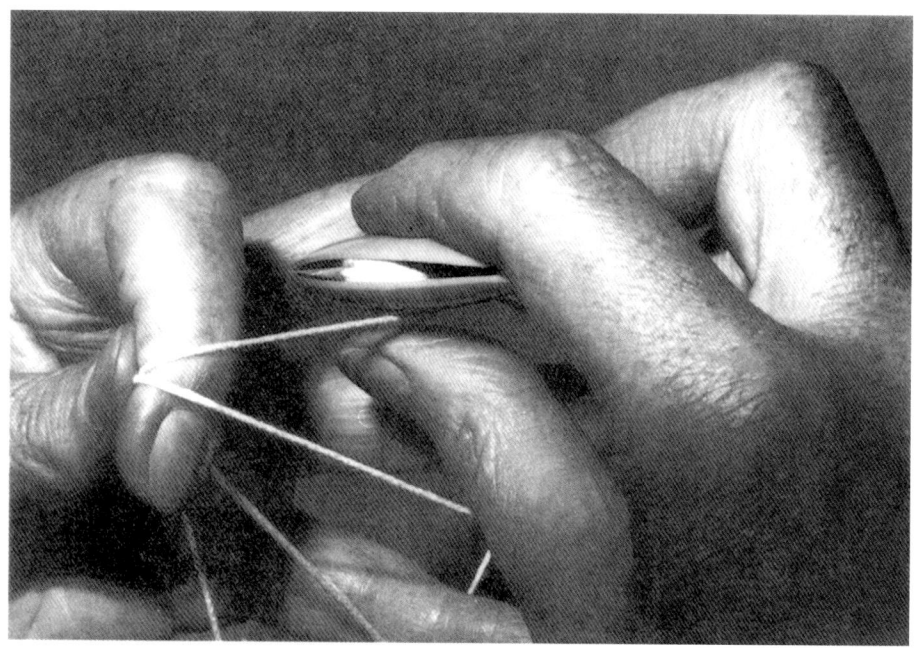

8 The thumb gets hold of the shuttle again behind the thread.

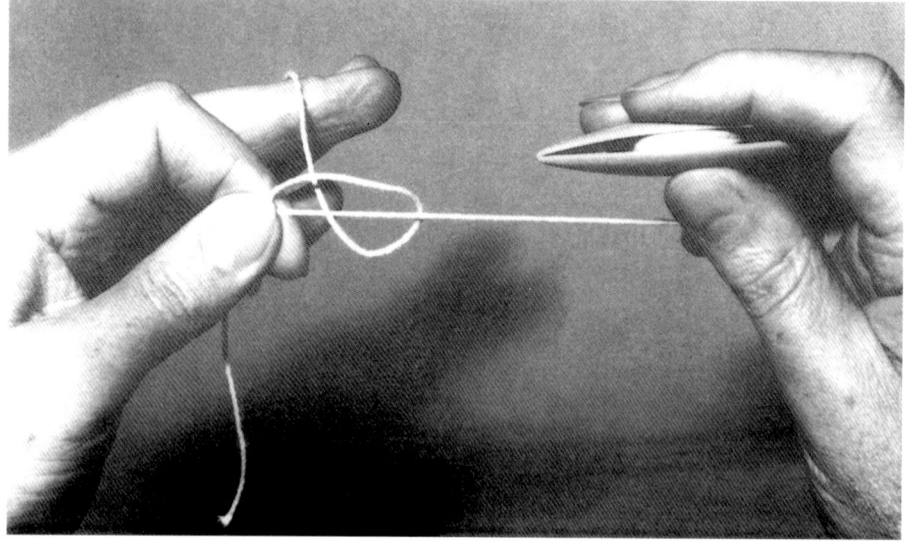

9 While taking the shuttle back to the right, again loosen the tension of the threadloop over the left hand and tighten the shuttle thread. The knot will flip over to the ring thread as before.

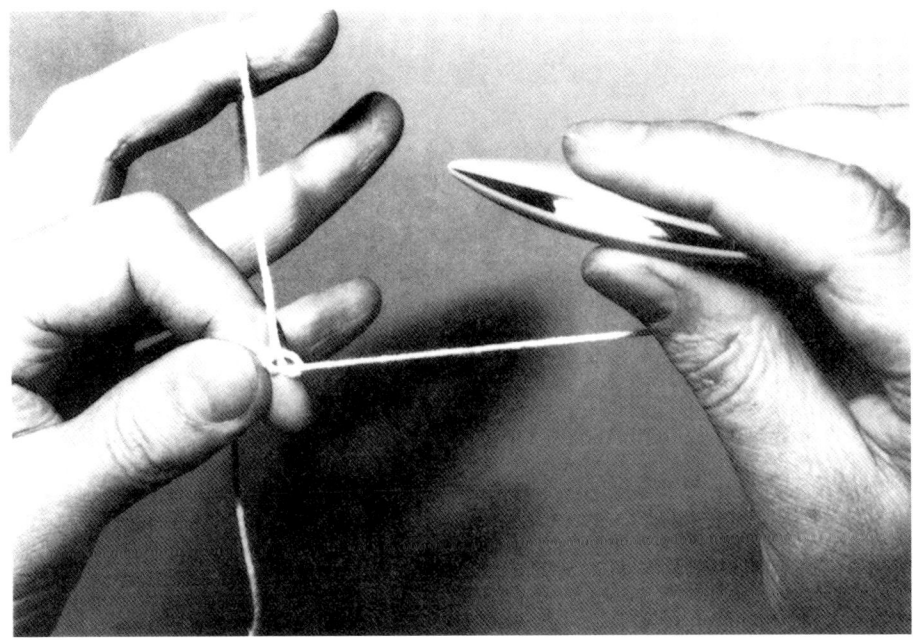

10 With lifting up your left middle finger slide the second half of the double knot towards your thumb.

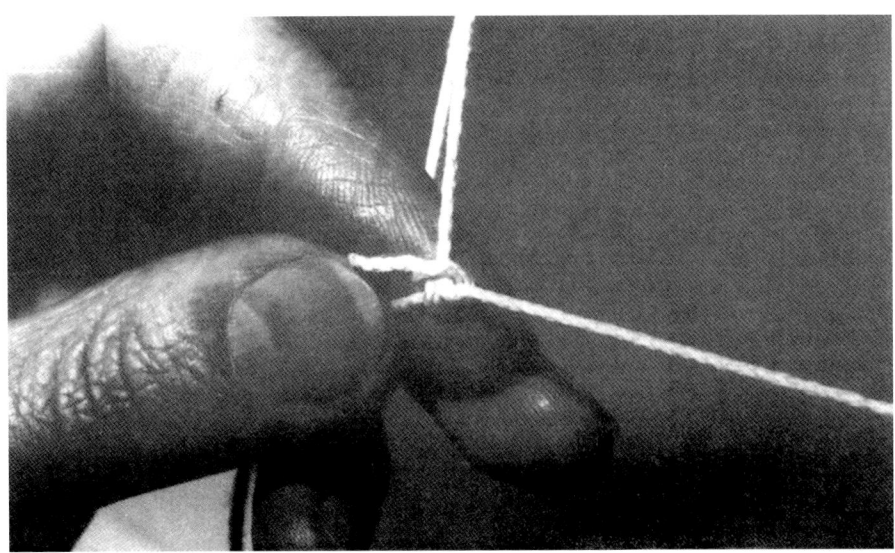

11 The finished double knot. It has a head and two legs through which you n move the core thread. – For closing the ring one pulls the shuttle thread to the right, to enlargen the loop over the hand, pull to the left.

IMPORTANT NOTE:

Traditional tatting patterns call these two half knots right knot and left knot. In other words, the left half is the right knot and the right half is the left knot.
So far, during my long experience with tatting, nobody has been able to explain to me the reasoning behind this. I will therefore allow myself with this introduction to innovative tatting to name the knots according to their position, that is, I will name the left half of the double knot *left* and the right half *right* knot.

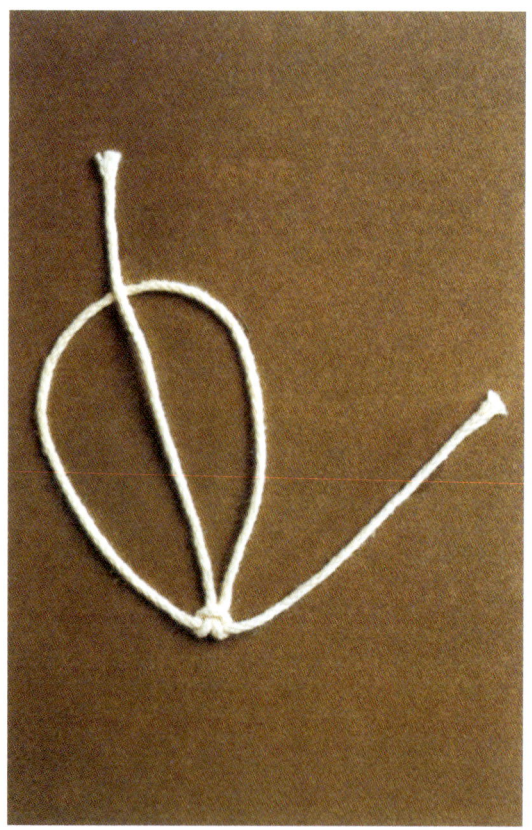 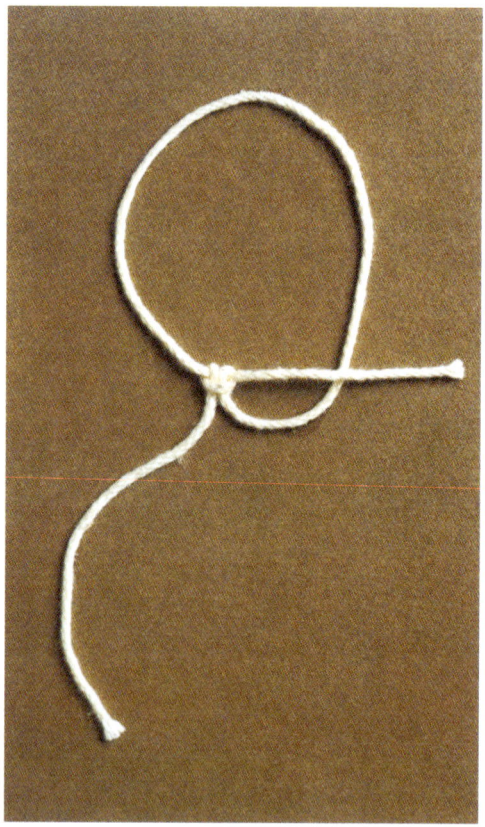

rs   To form a reverse stitch (rs) keep holding the bridge thread of the left hand tight while keeping the middle finger raised, make the exact same movement with the right hand and shuttle as shown above (photographs 1- 4 and 8 – 9). This knot basically stands upside down.

cs ½ ds + ½ rs make up the creative stitch (cs).

This stitch is being used   1. to start each work
                                                2. to add a new thread

ck The change knot (ck) is half of a stitch, that is: following a double stitch = ½ (right) cs and following a rs = ½ (right) ds

The change knot is used for a change in direction.

Jr If a ring consists of right knots only, this is called a Josephine ring (Jr).

Begin the Jr always with a ds which will not be counted. This will make the Jr lie flatter and not twisted

Example left:
10 count Jr = ring of 1 ds and 10 right knots

Examples center and right:
3 x 10 ct Jr = 3 Jr with 10 stitches worked closely after each other. Note that the 3rd Jr has been flipped backwards!

p Leaving a little space between two ds will form the picot (p) after the ring has been closed. *See photograph 12.*

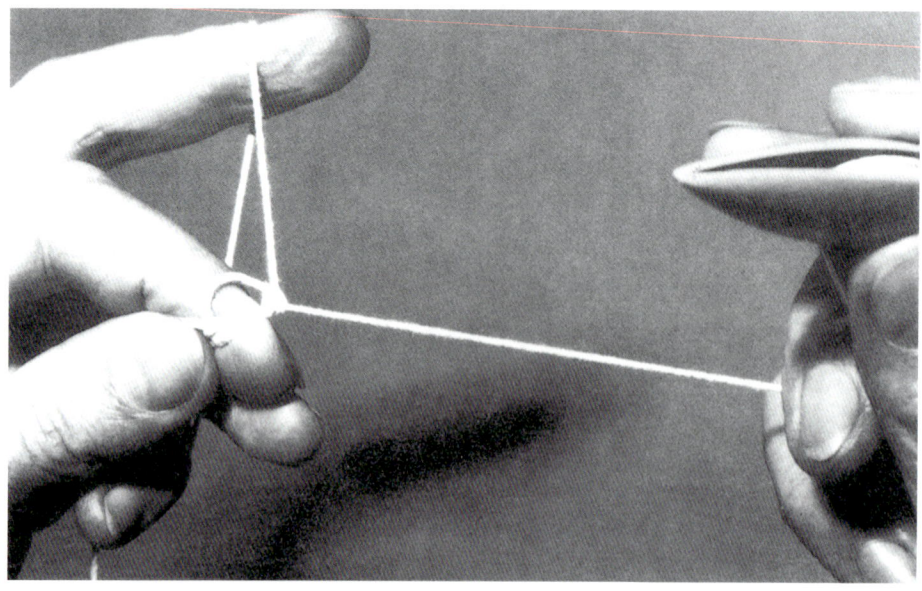

12

For closing a ring pull on the *shuttle thread* only while the left thumb holds the stitches.

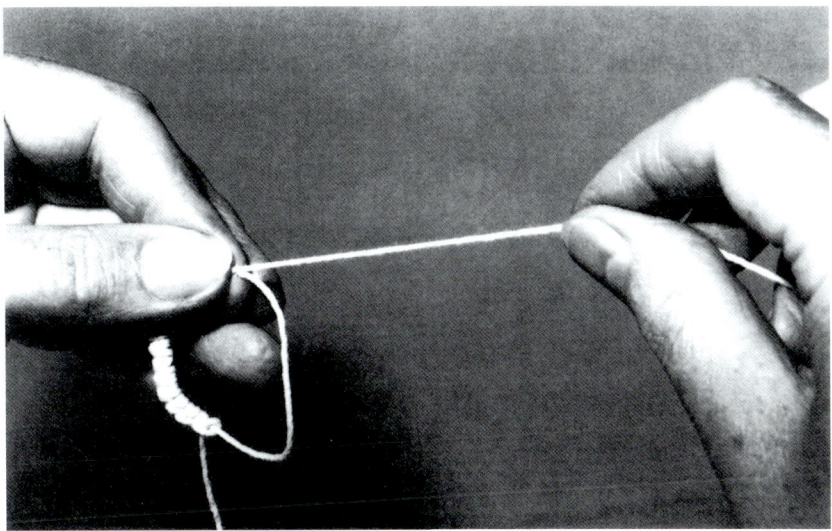

13 closing a ring.

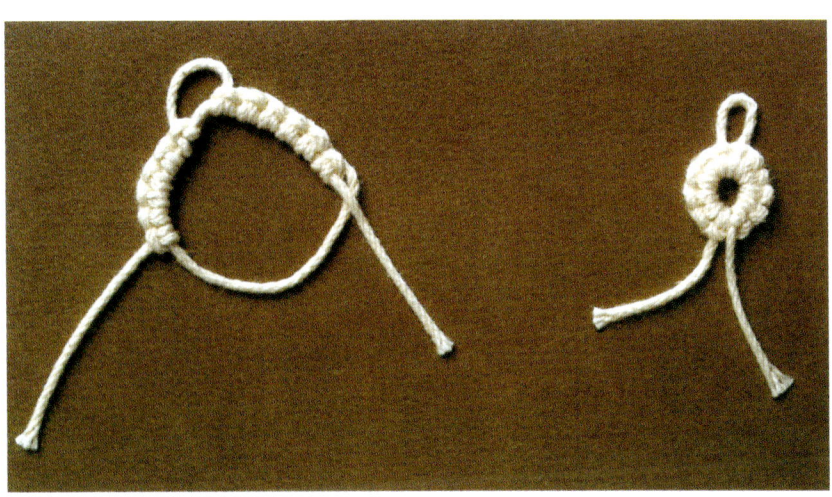

17

Pr Picot ring = a ring where each ds is separated by a picot.
Example:
10 ct Pr = ds, p, ds, p, ds, p, ds, p, ds, p, ds, p, ds, p, ds, p, ds, p, ds

3 x 10ct Pr = 3 Pr with 10 p each worked closely after each other. Note that the 2nd Pr has been flipped backwards!

Hint: for a 5 ct Pr the p should be about 3 mm large, the 7 ct Pr should have 5 mm p, and the 10 ct Pr should have about 1 cm long p.

WORKING WITH 2 AND 3 SHUTTLES

2 sh To work with rs, cs and ck a second shuttle will be necessary.

Grab hold of both thread ends with your left fingers. Lead one of the shuttle threads over the left hand and wrap it around your pinky a few times, then drop that shuttle to dangle freely. Use the second shuttle as described before.

The difference is that there will be no loop over your hand and no ring will be made.

In traditional tatting this is the manner how chains would be formed and for creative tatting it is used to work stems and stalks.

Hint: Beginners should start with this exercise because mistakes won't hinder the work. If one makes a mistake while working with only one shuttle, the rings can not be closed anymore and this may discourage the tatter.

3 sh For 3 shuttle work 2 threads will be laid over the left hand while working rs for stems and such. To work leaves and petals (as Jr and Pr) use the appropriate shuttle.

*Note: When working **rs** the stitches will be in the color of the shuttle that is held by the right hand!*

Change of Direction

In order to be able to place blossoms and leaves on both sides of a stem one will have to incorporate a change of direction:

This is no problem with 3 shuttle work. Just use the shuttle that holds the thread color that you want to use, work the called for Jr or Pr and place it as desired and then work the stem. While working with 2 shuttles one locks the work with a ck and turns before resuming with a Jr or Pr.

Adding New Thread

Wrap the old thread end a few times around your middle finger and hold the new thread together with the work in your left hand. Now work a cs with the new shuttle.

How to Open a Jr and Pr

There is usually no need for correction in creative tatting. Nature does not create with a ruler and pair of compass either. It does not matter at all if you are following a set pattern or not.

In traditional tatting it is very important to work correctly and count knots and picots carefully because a miscount would change the dimensions of the pattern repeat.

In order to open a ring grab hold of the last ds worked with thumb and forefinger of the left hand and carefully pull on the core thread as it comes out from the *first* knot, piece by piece. Ever so often stroke the knots from left to right until the loop is large enough again to accommodate the hand. A needle inserted between left and right knot can open up a ds. (open Jr accordingly).

Application to Ground Fabric

To appliqué pieces of creative tatting leave a 10 cm thread end at the beginning and end of the work. Pull these to the back of the ground fabric at the correct spot and tie a triple knot, then cut ends short.

Now the tatted pieces can be sewn on with a thin thread: Pr should be sewn with two stitches (at the lower and upper inner rim), picots will not be sewn on.

Apply Jr as desired, usually with just one stitch.

Stems should be stitched onto the fabric with a stitch every cm or so.

Note: If all your tatting has been worked correctly and very neat it will still come out with certain variations during the application to fabric. The p and the single elements stay relatively flexible. But again, no rulers or compasses used in nature! This is exactly what gives creative tatting the playful appearance and natural character.

INITIAL EXERCISES

The innovative patterns usually consist of:
> Picot rings (Pr)
> Josephine rings (Jr) and
> Reverse stitches (rs)

Do these few finger exercises before diving in:

1. Working picot rings (Pr) uses a relatively large amount of thread, that is, you have to keep pulling new thread. Try to do this using your pinky and ring finger of your left hand. Practice enlarging the loop of working thread over the left hand after each larger picot in this way. With time, this will become second nature.

2. Josephine rings consist merely of a number of right tatting knots. These too you should practice.

3. To form reverse stitches (rs), the thread over the left hand stays taught, this means only the right hand forms the stitches. – This might seem very unusual to the traditional tatting expert. – Practice using two colors and stitches as in the following example: 10 ds, 10 rs, 5 ds, 5 rs, 2 ds, 2 rs, 1 ds, 1 rs…

Exercises
Instructions
Finished Works

EXERCISES WITH PICOT RINGS

As a rule, start each work with a creative stitch (cs).

1ST ROW Flower: drop green sh,
5 ct Pr with red sh (small p)
Stem: red thread on left hand,
with green sh 10 rs, switch shuttles, ck, turn
Flower: 7 ct Pr (medium sized p)
Stem: red over left hand,
10 rs in green, switch shuttles, ck, turn
Flower: 10 ct Pr (large p)
Stem: red over left hand,
10 rs in green

2ND ROW Flower: 2 x 5 ct Pr, flip 2nd Pr over
Stem: 10 rs
Flower: 2 x 7 ct Pr, flip 2nd Pr over
Stem: 10 rs
Flower: 2 x 10 ct Pr, flip 2nd Pr over
Stem: 10 rs

3RD ROW Flower: 3 x 5 ct Pr, flip 2nd Pr over
Stem: 10 rs
Flower: 3 x 7 ct Pr, flip 2nd Pr over
Stem: 10 rs
Flower: 3 x 10 ct Pr, flip 2nd Pr over
Stem: 10 rs

Pattern Examples

a) cs
5 ct Pr with green sh
+ with pink thread on left hand work 5 rs with green sh
with green thread on left hand work 1 rs with pink
turn, 5 ct Pr with pink sh
with green thread on left hand work 1 rs, 5 ds in pink
drop pink shuttle, work 5 ct Pr with green sh
repeat from +

b) cs
5 ct Pr with green sh, turn
+ 5 ct Pr with red sh
with red thread on left hand work 1 cs, 5 rs in green
switch shuttles, 1/2 rs, drop red sh
5 ct Pr with green sh, turn
repeat from +

The same patterns can also be worked in the traditional tatting method (2nd solution):

a) cs
5 ct Pr with green
green on left hand, 5 ds, turn
5 ct Pr with red
red on left hand, 5 ds, turn

b) cs
5 ct Pr with red, turn
5 ct Pr with green
5 ds, turn

Traditional tatting experts will prefer the second way of tatting. But if you want to familiarize yourself with the principles of the creative tatting you should use the first method of tatting those flowers.

Place mats with Pr patterns.

MORE EXAMPLES

Yellow: single, double and triple picot rings of equal size were used here, they are:

a)   7 ct Pr

b)   10 ct Pr

Blue: All types of picot rings were used: single, double and triple as 5 ct, 7 ct or 10 ct Pr.

a) here the triplets are the flowers

b) here the triplets are the leaves

EXERCISES WITH JOSEPHINE RINGS

Jr Always begin a Jr with a double stitch (ds) but do not count this stitch.

	cs
flower bud:	drop green sh
	10 ct Jr with red sh
stem:	with red thread on left hand
	work 10 rs with green sh
flower buds:	drop green sh
	2 x 10 ct Jr with red
	flip 2nd Jr backwards
stem:	with red on left hand, 10 rs
flower buds:	2 x 10 ct Jr in red
stem:	red on left hand
	10 rs
flower buds:	3 x 10 ct Jr with red,
	flip 3rd Jr backwards
stem:	red on left hand
	10 rs, turn
leaf:	10 ct Jr in green,
	red on left hand
stem:	3 rs, turn
leaf:	10 ct Jr in green
stem:	with red on left hand
	10 rs, turn
leaves:	2 x 10 ct Jr,
	flip 2nd Jr backwards
stem:	with red on left hand
	10 rs, turn
leaves:	2 x 10 ct Jr in green
stem:	red on left hand
	10 rs, turn
leaves:	3 x 10 ct Jr with green,
	flip 3rd Jr backwards
	red thread on left hand,
	cs, turn
	3 x 10 ct Jr in green,
	flip 3rd Jr backwards
stem:	red on left hand
	10 rs

Pattern Examples

These patterns too can be worked in the traditional way of tatting. Try it out! But you will realize that pattern b) will be easier to work in the creative tatting method.

a) cs
drop purple sh, in pink 15 ct Jr
purple thread on left hand, 2 rs
drop pink sh, 15 ct Jr in purple, turn
pink thread on left hand, 5 rs
repeat from beginning

b) cs
drop dark purple sh
2 x 15 ct Jr in light purple, flip 2nd Jr backwards
light purple on left hand, 3 rs, turn
2 x 15 ct Jr in dark purple, flip 2nd Jr backwards
dark purple on left hand, 3 rs, turn
repeat from beginning

Pattern Examples

a) cs
3 x 15 ct Jr in variegated green, flip 3rd Jr backwards
lay thread over left hand, 5 green, not variegated, rs with 2nd sh
switch shuttles, ½ rs(ck), turn
repeat from beginning

b) cs
2 x 15 ct Jr in green, flip 2nd Jr backwards
1 x 10 ct Jr in red, flip backwards
with green thread on left hand, 3 ds with red sh
repeat from beginning

More examples with correct pattern repeats

a) Leaves: 5 ct Pr
   Buds: 10 ct Jr

b) Flowers: 5 ct Pr
   Leaves: 15 ct Jr

More appealing are mixed pattern repeats

a) Leaves: 7 ct Pr
   Buds: 15 ct J

b) Flowers: 7 ct Pr
   Leaves: 15 ct Jr

This type of tatting is much more relaxing because just basic principles have to be adhered to (e.g. the number of knots in Pr and Jr). Uneven distances between repeats of for instance the elements or whether you repeat a Pr or Jr once or twice completely depends on your taste.

a) Flowers: 10 ct Pr
   Leaves: 15 ct Jr
   Buds: 10 ct Jr

b) Leaves: 10 ct Pr
   Buds: 10 ct Jr
   Flowers: 7 ct Pr

Centerpiece with light purple tendril of picot rings and Josephine rings

Right page
A lavishly decorated garden tablecloth. This uses all creative tatting elements.

41

3 Shuttle Exercises

While working with 3 shuttles you will:

a) tat over two threads with the 3rd shuttle (for stems and branches) or
b) drop two shuttles,

	cs
stem:	with red and green thread (on left hand) tat over both with brown (sh in right hand) with 10 rs
leaf:	drop red and brown 1 x 5 ct Pr
stem:	work 5 brown rs over red and green thread, turn
leaf:	5 ct Pr
stem:	10 rs
buds:	3 x 10 ct Jr, flip 3rd Jr backwards
stem:	10 rs
leaves:	2 x 7 ct Pr, flip 2nd Pr backwards
stem:	10 rs
flowers:	3 x 5 ct Pr, flip 2nd Pr backwards
stem:	10 rs

Pattern Examples

a)   cs
     tat over orange and green with brown rs
     drop brown and orange sh, 3 x 15 ct Jr in green
     tat over orange and green with brown rs
     drop brown and green sh, 7 ct Pr with orange, etc.

b)   accordingly, but work leaves in Pr, buds (or grapes) in Jr

Pattern Examples

a)
	cs
leaves:	one, two or three 5 ct Pr
flowers:	1. 10 ct Pr plus
	15 ct Jr, flip this one backwards
	2. 7 ct Pr plus
	10 ct Jr, flip this one backwards

b)
	cs
leaves:	3 x 10 ct Pr
buds:	3 x 10 ct Jr
flowers:	1. 3 x 5 ct Pr
	2. 3 x 7 ct Pr
stem:	always tat over red and green thread with brown rs

CROCHETING OVER PICOT RINGS

You can work a closed leaf with crocheting over a picot ring (see below).

The top row shows 5 ct Pr as singles, doubles and triples.

In the second row, these Pr were over crocheted:

After closing the ring put the thread over the middle finger of the left hand and wrap around pinky (as in working with two sh), now crochet from picot to picot. At the end pull thread through the thread loop, place thread in front of the last rs (at stem) and work cs.

*Center piece with green tendril of leaves.
Elements for this pattern p. 48*

The elements for the centerpiece p. 47:

Instructions

Tie dark green, light green and green variegated threads together with 1 cs

Leaf study No. 1 (dark green)
10 ct Pr
crochet over (see p. 46)
1 rs over the other two threads
repeat twice

Leaf study No. 2 (light green)
2 x 7 ct Pr, flip 2nd Pr backwards, or
3 x 7 ct Pr, flip 3rd Pr backwards
(see p. 24)

Leaf study No. 3 (green variegated)
+) 3 x 15 ct Jr, flip 3rd Jr backwards
1 rs (with same sh), turn
repeat from +

Work 5 – 10 rs each in dark green over the two lighter threads between each leaf study (see p. 19).

Variations

Top 2 exercises, right page
Use of elements 2 and 3 (crocheted over 2)

Bottom 2 exercises, right page
Use of all three elements but in different color choices.

51

In creative tatting you can also work with pattern repeats instead of elements (see table runner below).

Instructions

for the brown table runner with ecru colored elements

	cs
Buds:	3 x 15 ct Jr (flip 3rd Jr backwards)
	cs
	3 x 15 ct Jr (flip 3rd Jr backwards)
	cs
stem:	9 rs
flowers:	3 x 7 ct Pr (flip 2nd Pr backwards)
	cs
stem:	15 rs
flower:	10 ct Pr, crochet over, cs
	in the corner motifs: repeat four times, repeat twice on long sides
stem:	15 rs
flowers:	3 x 7 ct Pr (flip 2nd Pr backwards)
	cs
stem:	9 rs
buds:	3 x 15 ct Jr (flip 3rd Jr backwards)
	cs
	3 x 15 ct Jr (flip 3rd Jr backwards)
	cs

Gathering of Picots

For working gathered picots it is important that the picots are not too small – and, more importantly, that they are of equal size. The number of picots or the size of the Pr depends on the thickness of the thread. In this case (perle cotton size 8) there are always 7 p per Pr.

How to do it: You will tie the picots (or some of the picots) to their own ring *before* closing the ring: pull the working thread through the (all or a part of the p) p with your crochet hook, lead the shuttle through this loop, seal with a right knot, tighten the loop and then close the ring.

7 ct Pr each, in single, double and triple form, all 7 p have been gathered

7 ct Pr each, (1, 2 and 3 fold), each only have 6 of the 7 p gathered

7 ct Pr each, (1, 2 and 3 fold), each only have 4 of the 7 p gathered

Pattern Examples

a) Leaf-Element: 15 ct Jr
   Flower-Elements: 7 ct Pr (the last 4 p are to be tied to the thread ring)
   (see p. 54)

b) Leaf-Elements: 7 ct Pr (as above)
   Flower-Elements: 3 x 5 ct Pr

Pattern Examples

a) Leaves: 3 x 7 ct Pr
   Buds:
   1. dark purple: 2 x 7 ct Pr (all p are gathered)
   2. light purple: 2 x 7 ct Pr (only the last 4 of the 7 p are gathered)

b) Leaves: 3 x 15 ct Jr
   Flowers:
   1. dark yellow: 3 x 7 ct Pr (all p are gathered)
   2. light yellow: 3 x 7 ct Pr (only the last 4 of 7 p are gathered)

Hint: the picots should be worked large and very even.

White center piece with yellow and green tendril

Flowers: dark yellow: 3 x 7 ct Pr (all 7 p are gathered)
light yellow: 3 x 7 ct Pr (gather only 4 p)

Leaves: green: 3 x 15 ct Jr

Stem: 5 – 15 rs (5 rs between leaf-elements each and otherwise 15 rs)

Ecru center piece with brown tendril

Work with two shuttles, that is: stems dark brown
Flowers, Leaves etc.: variegated brown.
The lighter parts of the variegated thread were used to work flowers and the darker parts to work the leaves. If there was a color break inside a Pr only the darker p were gathered

Pattern Examples

a) Leaf – elements: 5 ct Pr
    Flower – elements: 7 ct Pr (gather only the 4 last p)
    Pollen – element: 12 ct Jr

b) Leaf – elements: as above
    Flower – elements: as above
    Pollen – Element: as above

    Difference: for a) leaves and stems,
                  For b) stems and pollen were worked with the same thread

Ecru center piece with appliqués

Flower (mauve):	leave a 25 cm thread end and start with 1 x 10 ct Pr, over crocheted 2 rs (for this put shuttle over left hand and form knots with the thread end) repeat 4 times
Flower (variegated):	leave a 25 cm thread end and work 3 x 10 ct Pr
Leaves (dark green):	leave 25 cm thread end and begin with 7 ct Pr (gather before closing the ring) repeat twice
Leaves (med green):	begin after leaving a 25 cm thread end with 3 x 15 ct Jr rs with thread end over shuttle thread repeat twice
Leaves (light green):	leave 25 cm thread end and start with 3 x 20 ct Jr appliqué together with medium green leaves
Tendril (green variegated):	These are just 10 ct Jr that are worked closely to each other and automatically fall to the right or left side.

After finishing the elements always leave approximately 25 cm of thread ends on them, use these threads for your application to the ground fabric and seal with a triple knot.

To sew the elements down use a thinner thread preferably of similar color or in the color of the ground fabric, use stitches that go over the core thread because this one is covered by the knots (the stitches will be hidden).

Two Examples in Perle Cotton Size 5 (thicker)

Tendril with Blue Flowers: The leaves are 10 ct Pr done in green variegated thread.
Flowers are 15 ct Jr.

For the color change of the blossoms the new thread was added by means of a cs and both threads were cut after 10 cm. (thread ends were knotted on the back during appliqué).

Tendril with Red Flowers:

Work in the opposite way, that is, here the 10 ct Pr form the flowers and the 15 ct Jr make up the leaves. Here too use cs for adding a new colored thread.

Simple Elements of Creative Tatting

The following show simple tatting elements that can be combined or changed as you wish. In combination with stems and appropriate color choices more

variations are possible. They can of course also be appliquéd singly as shown here (to place mats etc.).

Christmas Tree

	cs
Top:	3 ct Pr
Trunk:	3 rs
Branches:	Ring (R) of: 5 ds, 1 small p, 4 larger p
	Ring (R) of: 4 large p, 1 small p, 4 ds
Trunk:	8 rs
Branches:	R of : 8 ds, 1 small p, 7 large p
	R of: 7 large p, 1 small p, 7 ds
Trunk:	8 rs
Branches:	R of: 12 ds, 1 small p, 11 large p
	R of: 11 large p, 1 small 1, 11 ds
Trunk:	30 rs, ck
	Fold last piece of trunk backwards at the center.

VARIATIONS OF THIS MAIN PATTERN:

1. work larger Pr, then the Christmas tree looks more stout
2. work more Pr, it will look larger
3. larger picots (they can even overlap)
4. cut open the picots

Herbaceous Plant with Orange Flowers
(opposite page, top left)

	Cs
Leaf:	3 x 10 ct Jr
Stem:	3 rs
Flowers:	2 x 5 ct Pr, flip 2nd Pr backwards
Stem:	5 rs, turn
Leaf:	3 x 10 ct Jr
Stem:	5 rs
Flowers:	2 x 7 ct Pr, flip 2nd Pr backwards
Stem:	7 rs, switch shuttles, ck
Leaf:	3 x 12 ct Jr
Stem:	15 rs, turn
Bottom Leaves:	1. ring: 5 large p + 10 ds
	2. ring: 10 ds + 5 large p
	flip second leaf backwards
Stem:	10 rs, turn
Leaves:	3 x 10 ct Jr
Stem:	3 rs
Buds:	2 x 10 ct Jr
Stem:	3 rs
Leaf:	1 x 10 ct Jr
	1 green rs to finish

Herbaceous Plant with Blue Buds
(opposite page, top right)

Work like the previous one but in reverse manner, that is, here the leaves are Pr and the buds are Jr.

Herbaceous Plant with Yellow Flowers
(opposite page, top left)

	cs
Flower:	5 ct Pr
Stem:	5 rs, turn
Leaves:	2 x 12 ct Jr, flip 2nd Jr backwards
Stem:	5 rs
Flowers:	2 x 7 Pr, flip 2nd Pr backwards
Stem:	5 rs
Leaves:	3 x 12 ct Jr
Stem:	5 rs
Flowers:	2 x 7 ct Pr, flip 2nd Pr backwards
Stem:	15 rs, turn
Bottom Leaves:	1. ring: 5 large p + 10 ds 2. ring: 10 ds + 5 large p flip second leaf backwards
Stem:	10 rs, turn
Leaves:	3 x 10 ct Jr
Stem:	3 rs, switch shuttles, turn
Leaves:	3 x 10 ct Jr
Stem:	3 rs, switch shuttles, ck
Leaves:	3 x 10 ct Jr 1 green rs to finish

Herbaceous Plant with Purple Buds
(opposite page, top right)

Work like previous one but in reverse manner, that is, here the leaves are Pr and the buds are Jr.

71

Flowers

Blossom:	leave 30 cm of thread at start
	+ 3 x 12 ct Jr, shuttle thread on left hand, work cs with thread end,
	repeat twice from +
	cut thread after about 30 cm
Stem:	hold blossom with thumb and forefinger of left hand, take both thread ends on left hand, add green thread and work rs until enough stem is made
Leaf:	5 ct Pr
Stem:	as many rs as you like

Bunch of Flowers

Blossoms:	as above work several blossoms (example shows 6 from different variegated threads)
	cut green thread also only after 30 cm
Stem:	combine all threads and knot over them with green rs

Small Bouquet

Consists of 5 separately worked flowers and 3 separately worked leaves that were bunched together with a stem. A second possibility: work all stems a bit longer and tie together at crossing points with green thread – this thread could be sewn to the back for appliqué.

Flower:	leave 30 cm of thread
	3 x 10 ct Pr, flip 2nd Pr backwards
Stem:	hold flower, add green thread, flower thread over left hand, some rs in green, cut green and yellow threads after 30 cm
Leaf:	knot two green threads together with cs
	drop 1 shuttle, with the other sh work
	3 x 12 ct Jr, flip 3rd Jr backwards
Stem:	add 2nd sh, cs, 5 rs, turn
Leaf:	+) 3 x 12 ct Jr, flip 3rd Jr backwards, rs, turn
	3 x 12 ct Jr, flip 3rd Jr backwards
Stem:	add 2nd sh, as many rs as desired
Leaf:	if desired as in +)

Finish: take all threads over left hand and work rs over them

Traditional Tatting

Rings (work with 1 sh) and chains (work with 2 sh) form the elements of the pattern repeats of traditional tatting. Picots can be used for connecting rings with each other and otherwise for decoration. They should always be worked even in size.

To connect a ring to a ring:

At the appropriate spot (denoted in pattern with a +) pull the working thread of the left hand through the correct picot with your crochet hook and lead your shuttle through this loop. Lifting of the middle finger will close this loop and the connection can be sealed with ½ ds.

Simultaneously attaching to fabric:

Pull the core thread through the fabric with your crochet hook, lead shuttle through this loop, tighten loop and work ½ ds to seal.

Next, a few Instructions:

1a	CH:	7 ds, attach
1b	CH:	3 ds, p, 3 ds, attach
2a	CH:	3 ds, small p, large p, small p, 3 ds, attach
2b	CH with ring:	3 ds, with left sh: ring of 5 ds 3 ds, attach (one could also work a Jr instead of a ring)
3a	Ch with R: With left sh:	4 ds 3 ds, p, 3 ds (= 3 – 3), 4 ds, attach
3b	CH: R: CH:	5 ds 3 – 1 – – 1 – 3 5 ds, attach

1a   1b

2a   2b

3a   3b

4 – 6 TWO COLOR PATTERNS

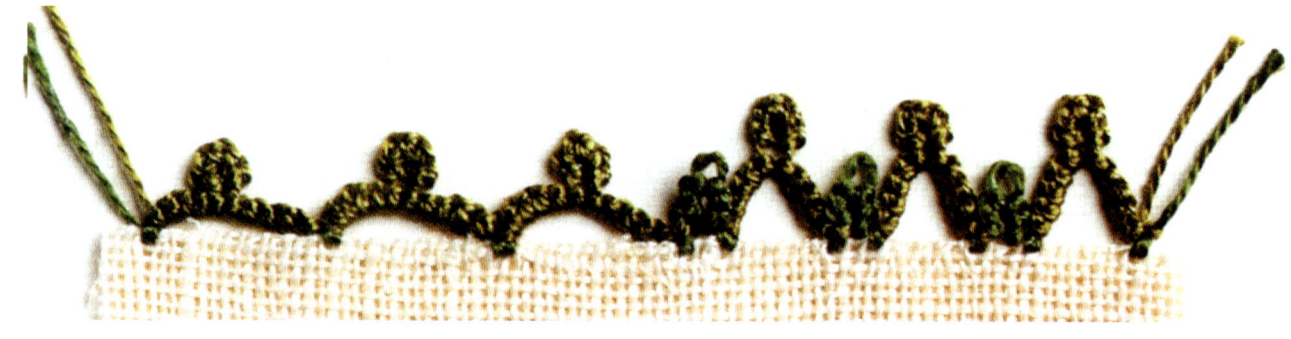

4a	4a	CH:	7 ds, attach	4b
		R:	5 ds from core thread, attach	
	4b	CH:	7 ds, attach	
		R:	3 – 3, attach	

5a	5a	CH with R:	5 ds	5b
		with left sh:	R of 5 ds	
			5 ds, attach	
	5b	R and	R: 3 – 3, attach	

6a	6a	R:	4 – 4 – 4 – 4, turn	6b
		CH:	4 – 4, turn	
			(from 2nd R on, work joins instead of p – notation: 4 + 4 – 4 – 4)	
	6b	R:	4 – 4 – 1 – – 1 – 4 – 4, turn	
		CH:	4 – 4, turn	

EDGE WORK WITH THE CS
(gold on left hand, red in right hand)

- **7a** ½ ds, ½ rs (always alternating, attach when desired)
- **7b** 1 ds, ½ rs (always alternating, attach when desired)
- **7c** 2 ds, ½ rs (always alternating, attach when desired)
- **7d** 1 ds, 1 rs (always alternating, attach when desired)

LACE WITH 1 SHUTTLE *(can be sewn on afterwards)*

8a-c   8a   R: 4 – 8 – 4
                     (from 2nd R on: work joins instead of picots)
                     (4 + 8 – 4)
              8b   R: 4 – (+) 4 – 4 – 4
              8c   R: 4 – (+) 4 – 1 – – 1 – 4 – 4

9   9   R: 4 – (+) 4 – 4 – 4, turn
                     always repeat

10   10   R: 4 – (+) 4 – 4 – 4, turn
                     R: 5 – 5, turn
                     R: 4 + 4 – 4 – 4, turn
                     R: 4 + 4 – 1 – – 1 – 4 – 4, turn
                     R: 4 + 4 – 4 – 4
                     R: 5 + 5, turn